FOREVER NOW

A Journey to Awakening

MATEO MADANI

FOREVER NOW

Light Books Publishing
Honolulu, Hawaii

Copyright © 2008 by **Mateo Madani**

Published by: Light Books Publishing
Honolulu, Hawaii 96826 U.S.A.
www.LightBooksPublishing.com
Email: info@LightBooksPublishing.com

All rights reserved. No part of this book may be reproduced by any mechanical, photographic, or electronic process, or in the form of a phonographic recording; nor may it be stored in a retrieval system, transmitted, or otherwise be copied for public or private use—other than for "fair use" as brief quotations embodied in articles and reviews without prior written permission of the publisher.

Library of Congress Control Number: 2008933529

ISBN 978-0-9746278-8-5

Editor: Kiran Ramchandran

Cover Design by: Neal Izumi

First Printing, August 2008

Printed in the United States of America

CONTENTS

ACKNOWLEDGMENTS	vi
1 AWAKENING BEGINS	11
2 WHEN THE WORST THINGS ARE THE BEST	35
3 WHAT CAUSES OUR DOWN FALL?	67
4 THE POWER OF LISTENING	79
5 THE ART OF SURRENDER	95
6 THE SECRET OF SELF-LOVE	111
7 THE EGO	119
8. THE MYSTERIOUS COIN	133
9 FOREVER NOW: SAVOR THE PRESENT	139

ACKNOWLEDGMENTS

I would like to thank my sister, Fahemeh, who is the general manager of my hotel and restaurant, Casa De Mateo, in Montreal, Canada, for her unflinching support and commitment. Thank you for believing in me and making it possible for me to offer my teachings to the world.

I thank my daughters, Tierra, Estrella and Oceana for their understanding. You were deprived of my presence during the initial stages of my awakening, yet we have maintained a close relationship. I have not been with you as much as I should have been. My nieces, Azalia and Elena who have been like my own children. I derive tremendous joy from having you all in my life.

And of course, my dear Kathleen, who has contributed enormously to this book, from its conception. Her love, understanding, patience and support have been of great help to me.

I thank Tina Quizon for inspiring me to start writing, and for interviewing me and transcribing the first manuscript.

A special thanks goes to my good friend, Macario Rodriguez, who has been singing and performing in my restaurant for twenty years; Ann Marie Parant, who has been taking care of my seminars and retreats; Louise Bergeron one of my most dedicated students and a friend; and Jim Henderson for his friendship and support.

I thank Ganshet Nandoskar for inspiring and encouraging me to start giving seminars again. You have been a supportive friend. I also thank his wife, Andrea for her compassion. Thank you to Mathieu Paquet, for all your contributions to the retreat; and to my student, Michael Beau Bates for helping proofread the manuscript. Thank you to all the others who have been supportive.

A big Thank You to the team of professionals at Light Books Publishing: The developmental editor, Leanne Trapedo Sims; final editor, Kiran Ramchandran; and cover designer, Neal Izumi.

Lastly, a special Thank You to Dr. Zeal Okogeri for recognizing the potential of this book. Your inexhaustible energy and enthusiasm made it possible.

DEDICATION

My greatest desire is for people to get along. I dedicate this book to those individuals who are truly making that happen.

# One

Awakening Begins

How the AWAKENING process begins…

There is an old fable about a young chicken and a mother hen that lived peacefully on a country farm.

One day, the chick ran to her mother in fear. "Momma, I overheard the farmer talking. He said he was going to hire somebody to tear down the farm. He's going to destroy our home!"

Forever Now

The mother hen remained calm. "Don't worry, my dear, there is no way our home will be destroyed."

Three days passed. On the fourth day, the little chick again came running to her mother, "Momma, I overheard the farmer talking with three strange men. They said they were going to help him tear down our farm. They're going to destroy our home, Momma! We're doomed!"

Again, the mother hen put her child at ease. "Do not worry, my dear, nothing is going to happen to our home. We're going to be okay."

Early the next morning, the little chick again came sprinting home gripped in utter panic. "Momma, I heard the farmer tell his family of a different plan. Now he's decided that he is going to tear down the farm himself."

Suddenly, the mother hen froze in fear. Her eyes turned sharp with worry. "My sweet dear, pack up your things immediately. It's time for us to get out of here."

The duo made haste. They quickly escaped down the dried river road.

Confused, the little chick finally beseeched her mother, "Momma, why are we leaving now? You always told me we didn't have to worry."

"That all changed, my sweet dear, because the farmer made a most powerful decision," the mother hen patiently explained. "Whenever you depend on others, there is only a tiny chance that something will ever happen. But when you decide to do something yourself, there's a greater possibility that things will happen fast."

Your Awakening is in your own hands!

Awakening is a result of your own desire, perseverance, practice and hard work. Awakening is reached only by your true willingness to catalyze change within yourself. It involves accepting full responsibility for your present state of being. This means courageously confronting the way your life has turned out, while also admitting to the causes and reasons that may have led it to waver from the path of your intended hopes and dreams.

Total self-responsibility is a concept that many of us find difficult to accept. We fail to claim true responsibility for our situations because our ego, often nourished by our insecurities, provides an illusionary sense of self-protection. In our human frailty, we desperately cling to this feeling of false protection that all too often manifests itself in blame. We point fingers at others believing them to be at fault for the troubles in our own lives.

We blast our accusations far and wide, sparing no ground from personal to existential: Why was I born in this country? Why am I living in this city? Why did I end up with such incapable parents? Why did I end up with such selfish friends? Why doesn't my boyfriend or girlfriend ever understand me? Why am I stuck with this job? Why do I have such a lousy boss, manager, contractor or secretary?

The questions become infinite. They spiral into a quagmire of chaos and confusion. Our minds forever remain hampered by this pattern of thought, until one day, there is clarity.

Examine your relationships as the reflections of what you are.

If you find yourself dealing with an individual who is full of anger or resentment, realize that whatever level of anger or resentment he or she is expressing is more than likely the exact level of anger or resentment that you are holding on to.

If your sons or daughters are not as appreciative of your efforts as you expect them to be, realize that this is exactly how you have performed in the past. The same goes for your wife, husband, boyfriend, girlfriend, or boss. If you look at your life carefully and objectively, you will see that you yourself have exhibited this same kind of behavior towards others. The way you treated some other relationship is more than likely the same way this current relationship is treating you. Sometimes we search far and wide for answers that are often right in front of us. The people around

Forever Now

us are mirrors showing us exactly who were are, who we were, and who we will become until we take control. If you want to look at your life and where you are at this moment, take a look at your relationships. Look at the people around you. That will give you a good picture. The universe provides clues to our lives through our relationships.

In order to transcend the realm of mirror reflections with people, you need to lift yourself beyond your negative emotions. Until you are able to release yourself from your fear, anger, resentment, jealousy, and greed, your actions and reactions in life will continually suffer their debilitating influence.

The moment you are elevated by a level of understanding based on compassion and love, you will find that your experiences will seem to have dramatically shifted. But this change will occur only when total acceptance of who you truly are is realized.

Fear is most often our most crippling emotion. It prevents us from reaching a state of awakening. For example, in some situations, you may feel stuck in your relationship because you are paralyzed by a fear of an unknown future. Consequently, you remain in your comfort zone and complain instead of acting. You can stay in your uncomfortable situation and learn from it for the sake of self-evolution and spiritual growth, or you can extricate yourself and search for more favorable experiences. The choice is yours. Either way you are awakening.

My personal journey…

I remember celebrating the opening of my twelfth restaurant. It was an extravagant affair that should have swept me away with tides of joy and excitement.

But it didn't.

Instead, I remember sitting in the corner of the dining room feeling the darkness of the night swallowing me in loneliness. The world as I knew it began to recede from me. I felt suddenly alone, existing only within the edges of my breath.

Forever Now

The excitement of the event vanished from my heart. It wasn't that I was unappreciative or misguided; in fact, I felt a sudden truth:

Emptiness.

Was this all there was to life— the pursuance of material successes? The collection of personal accolades?

My emptiness began to frame a singular fear… death.

Here I am: a successful, healthy, and prosperous man with a near-perfect family. I have a beautiful wife, two lovely children and a triumphant realm of prospering restaurants.

Is this who I am? Or is this but a series of reflections of what I think I should be? Only death and it's penetrating presence seemed real to me. It was absolute. It contained truth, while my life, and my living of it, seemed built on illusions. I was relating to death with a life that did not contain the same level of truth. A crippling fear arose from the darkness settling itself within the spaces of my harrowing emptiness.

As that night progressed, I began to unravel. I became obsessed with death. My thoughts shifted from happiness—the warmth of my family—the power of my business—into a cauldron of anxiety. An unfamiliar heaviness descended upon me.

I remember not knowing what was happening to me. I was descending, spiraling with no one to confide in. Emotions began cascading, confusing me with dizzying alarm.

Who am I? What's happening to me?

I began to drink more. At the time, I had no access to what I considered "spirituality."

I almost died one night from drinking.

The thoughts in my head were thick and suffocating. I could

Forever Now

neither escape them nor find a way out from them.

Soon after, I decided to take off for South America. I needed to do this. I didn't know why. I was buoyed only by instinct. I left everything behind. I had no map of where I was going, but for the first time, I was completely unconcerned with my business and my family.

Once I arrived in South America and checked into a hotel, I didn't leave my bed. I was exhausted. I simply stared vacantly at the ceiling fan. After days of inertia, I finally found a semblance of life-force and left my room. I made my way to the restaurant and realized that I couldn't remember the last time I'd eaten.

When the meal arrived, my body had no joy for it. Everything tasted like poison. The tables around me were filled with people laughing, eating, sharing wine and warm conversation, but the noise scratched too acute in my ears. The colors were dizzyingly intense. My senses were slipping. My balance and composure were frayed into oblivion.

I returned to my room and found great solace in its emptiness.

A few days later, I again found the courage to step out of the confines of my hotel room. I wandered aimlessly through the streets, enjoying total anonymity. I was suddenly struck by a psychic pain possessing little logic, yet containing a very painful primal feeling: why is no one paying attention to me?

Then I saw a man without legs propelling himself through the streets with his hand. The image of him gripped me. It was as if he possessed some unseen force. Or perhaps I did. I didn't know. I felt a magnetic force compelling me to follow him. I was suddenly exhilarated by an incredible amount of energy stemming from compassion.

Overwhelmed by compassion, I handed this man all my money and returned to my hotel room. That night, tears ran rivers from my eyes. I moved between eerie calm and dark ruminations.

Forever Now

Something was happening to me. I was on a precipice of bold and powerful changes. Though I could sense it, I was still so very unsure as to its direction and purpose.

I didn't see solutions to my problems in spite of the fact that I am a fairly intelligent and successful member of society. My undefined state was unbearable. My stability was lost. I didn't know what to grab onto. So I grabbed onto nothing.

I just felt the deluge of emotions consuming me—emotions that vacillated between peace and flashes of anxiety. Eventually, desperation overwhelmed me. I desired to let go of everything.

I looked for a way to end my life and surrender to death.

The next day, I once again left the hotel room, but this time I took solace on a rock at the beach. A lady approached me.

"Hi," she said.

I turned and stared at her without uttering a word. She joined me on the rock. Together we lost our gaze upon the infinite ocean.

A few minutes passed.

"Are you alright?" she asked. I still didn't answer. "I've seen you around for the past few days," she pressed, "I've sort of been watching you. Is everything okay?"

I noticed a book in her hand. Her eyes caught mine, and then she asked if she might read an excerpt for me.

I acquiesced without much preference either way.

She began reading aloud, and almost immediately, the words made their fix on me. With every one of her words, my mind and body shifted. The sensation was subtle but powerful. I shook with excitement. The words falling from her lips were all new territory for me. I felt like a child. The book was by Deepak

Chopra. It's truth was simple. I became thirsty for every page, and swallowed every sentence and idea she fed me.

I remained gripped in that moment until she finished reading the passage.

The woman read another book to me. She spoke to me about the spiritual world. My journey became entwined with hers. She invited me to travel with her to Sedona, Arizona.

That was my first encounter with a spiritual teacher.

Over the course of time, this woman began to help me, feeding me knowledge, and guiding my journey.

FACING DEATH IN SEDONA

I eventually left South America and followed her back to the States. She took me on a tour of a beautiful canyon in

Sedona. I was full of adventurous exuberance. When the path we traversed ended, I forged far ahead of everyone else. I hiked down the narrow precarious side of a cliff. About halfway down, I froze.

Fear paralyzed me. I stood immobile, sweating, and fastened to the ground like glue. I was unable to take even the tiniest of steps. I was completely overwhelmed because I was shaken by the fierce realization that this exact location had appeared in my dreams countless times.

I tasted a unusual bitterness in my throat; it was death.

My thoughts began to float...

I am here, at the exact place, where I have imagined my demise—dreamt about my death. I am here to confront my end.

Suddenly gaining an omnipresent perspective, I found myself

floating over my own body. I saw myself catapulting over the cliff. I sailed like a forlorn bird into the deeps of the canyon. I hit the ground without mercy.

I closed my eyes. I surrendered. This was the moment of my death.

I saw it. I felt it. I accepted it. And now I am free from it. Free from its fear.

Time passed and I had no idea how long I had been rooted to the edge. At some point, I opened my eyes, and returned up the narrow cliff trail. My legs started to shudder violently. Adrenaline, shock and a torrent of emotions crushed me. I fell to the earth.

After a prolonged recovery, our group descended out of the canyon. As we reached the end of the trail, I was besieged by laughter! Euphoria infused every cell of my being! A feeling of lightness then catapulted me into exhilaration. To this day, that feeling of joy is indelibly etched into my memory.

I was reborn. My process of awakening had just begun.

The following day, we traveled to see a great sage who also resided in Sedona, Arizona. When I met him, I was unable to speak. My mouth found no words, but my thoughts suddenly became unobstructed by worldly emotion. I felt like an open vessel of mind and soul. Seated before this man, I could only look deeply into his eyes. Our transference of communication was limited to this avenue, yet it seemed infinite in its sharing. We spoke only with our eyes. Only silence.

After our time had reached conclusion, I was approached by one of his disciples.

"What did you talk about?" she asked.

"Nothing," I responded.

Forever Now

She was shocked, unable to understand how I could have possibly made this pilgrimage from South America on my return to Canada only to share a moment of silence with her Master.

What she did not comprehend was that this "moment of silence" was an invaluable gift from her Master. Within those minutes, her master gave me the space to discover that the truth of my awakening was within me. I had the power.

We all possess it. My thoughts, when freed, were able to open the doors to a far deeper understanding of myself and others than what could be achieved by words alone.

The silence that I shared with the Master was powerful in that it helped me discover a lack of wanting inside me. I was left completely blank, but not empty. Simply said, for the first time, I was devoid of inner noise.

My lack of want persisted for several years.

From that moment forward, I acted with an absence of self-interest. I also possessed an absence of expectation.

I finally began to understand that in order to be born—awakened—I had to go through a step of dying.

Sometimes awakening is a gentle process.

Other times it is a very intense experience, similar to my own, and it can be made even more arduous because of our own stubbornness. Sometimes, our strength can be our weakness. Our strong wills refuse to surrender to the burgeoning feelings of truth that signal the beginning of the awakening process. When we fight the change, the process of awakening turns more grueling, or even worse, it is never realized.

I had to be hit hard in order to get to this stage of development. In the past, I was moving aimlessly from one thing to another. I had no idea what I was looking for, no intuition.

Forever Now

The emptiness I felt the night of my restaurant's celebration became the impetus that led me toward change. I learned that I needed to "go inward;" to look sincerely within myself and confront the delusion, lies, attachments, and selfishness that had not only been guiding my actions and reactions, but had also defined my very identity.

In the end, I learned that it is those polluted feelings and emotions that shape our perspective, not just of our world but also of ourselves.

Our thoughts are constantly governed by the influence of those emotions. They own us, until we cleanse ourselves of them.

My return to my family and business.

I felt I was ready to rejoin my place in the community, the home and life that I had built and cherished for so many years. But, I quickly found that this was not the case. Upon my return, I was unable to function.

I could not endure even a moment in my business. I continued to feel numb and empty. I remembered wandering the downtown area aimlessly, lost inside myself. The changes that occurred within me were not compatible with my previous existence.

My awakening process made me even less connected to the life I had previously built because it was changing my values at a fundamentally core level.

I knew I needed to continue my journey forward. There was no turning back. It was time to fully embrace the awakening process.

So, what is an Awakening?

There comes a time in everyone's life when you look inward for the answers. This is the beginning of the "Awakening" process. It is a catalyst for change and celebration. It is a joyous occasion. Awakening is activated when one contemplates deeply and starts asking the following questions:

Forever Now

Who am I?

What is my relationship to the world?

Is this all there is to life?

Awakening can be a paradox. You may imagine it as a state of bliss. And though achieving it may mean your arrival to a higher state, the journey to get there is demanding, painful, and frightening.

I know from my own experience that awakening can assault the consciousness on every level:

- Feelings of emptiness, even if you have fame and fortune.
- A loss of confidence
- Heaps of wondering
- Agitation
- Loss of interest in the world of activity.

The awakening process can be long, confusing, and painful with persistent feelings of ups and downs. Strange as it may seem, this emotional roller coaster is actually the process by which big steps forward are made.

As you read this book, allow the stirring up of your conscious state and gradually move toward awakening.

 Two

When the Worst Things Are the Best Things

Change is up to you. When you choose change, you invite boldness into your life. The time for talk and indecision ends. There is no external element—nothing 'out there' that you need to seek in order to initiate change. Not a new friend, a new job, a new home, or a change of scenery will ever be the impetus. You need only to seek and summon your own heart's desire.

Forever Now

Nothing beyond yourself allows you to seize change.

Presently, your life may feel overwhelmed by an inordinate amount of pressure. You may sense limitation and constriction. You may find yourself weakened or paralyzed by insecurity. You may be unable to act with determination and conviction. In essence, you may find you are unable to access the path toward happiness because ultimately, you don't have the tools to free yourself from the levels of stress that are hamstringing your true potential and spirit.

Think for a moment. Allow for a switch in perspective.

Could this cauldron of consuming emotions actually be a sign of hope?

Take another step. Make a mental shift.

Believe that hope is in the air and you will no longer have the desire or need to remain a slave to insecurity and fear. Change and hope are here. They are within you. Adjusting your thoughts and beliefs allow you to claim them and free yourself in your work, your relationship, or any of life's distresses.

All you have to do is wake up.

Awaken yourself and remember that this is not your home. This is not your origin. Our stay on earth is only temporary. Imagine you have nothing to lose, and realize you have nothing to fear.

Boldness is the road to happiness and freedom.

Put faith in your feelings and intuition. Turn your ear inward—contemplate!

An alternate path is at your fingertips. Let clarity be your guide—the clarity obtained from a deep trust in your own feelings and instincts.

This path will allow you to recognize possibilities you previously dismissed due to old patterns of emotional and mental blockages.

This understanding is the first step towards the gateway of new opportunities. This trust in self is the most positive action you need to undertake.

Take another step forward.

Right now, replace doubt with determination. Make no excuses. Move forward boldly. Hesitation is a form of fear.

This step is not easy. It is difficult to cast off our false protective instincts—those that are propagated by fear and insecurity. But remember, the feeling of safety these emotions create is illusionary. Not only do these subversive emotions not protect us, but they also keep us hostage to our imagined limitations.

You must remember that you alone imposed these conditioned responses on yourself. But you have the power to reverse it because you are the source. All ceasing and starting begins and ends with you. It is all in accordance with the power of your will.

I don't believe that there are any accidents or coincidences in life. You are reading this book for a reason. It has come to you at the right moment. Do the words resonate?

I suggest you read this book slowly so that the ideas, themes, and practices are allowed to seep into your awareness. Allow them to become comfortable in your mind before moving on to the next practice. Let your mind digest and work toward its own conclusions so that it alone moves you forward. This book is not your shepherd. You are your own guide. Give your instincts the permission to assume that role.

Begin to practice this wisdom until it is second nature. It is not complicated or esoteric. Your practice begins now. Now is always the potent moment.

Previously, I mentioned that perhaps you might be facing a present life of stress, disharmony and dissatisfaction. I suggested

Forever Now

a switch in perspective where these ailing elements could be seen instead as a sign of hope and change. Now I would like to take that line of thought further:

The recognition of unhappiness is your soul's signal that immediate change is necessary because you are negating what you really love.

To get what you really love, seize the opportunity for change. Buoy yourself with confidence from your instincts and feelings and act with that clarity. Translate it into abundant energy. Clarity and energy signify that you are mindful of the present moment.

Clarity and energy are the master keys to success, allowing us the material and spiritual freedom we seek.

Act, decide, and commit instead of running in circles. Repetition, like hesitation, is another form of fear.

When you are in the midst of a demanding and delicate

situation, impatience and self-doubt visit. Remember that these are our false methods of protecting ourselves.

Recall the wisdom: Fortune favors the bold one.

Why are the worst things also the best things?

When you are deeply troubled, touched by tragedy and pain, all the wisdom in the world makes no impact. It doesn't penetrate and it seems evasive. Instead, you react to negative circumstances with equal negativity from a space of selfishness, greed, and attachment. You blame yourself and others. You cling to your comfort zone for protection. Consequently, you stagnate and become bored. This boredom offends the soul. Beneath the boredom, you unconsciously seek change.

Attachment is a form of stagnation.

The soul is uncomfortable with stagnation. Stagnation blocks clarity in the same way a stagnant body of water becomes murky with debris.

Forever Now

There is intelligence beyond the mind—soul—that will force you to change your direction and course of life. The higher mind can address your soul's purpose. You can access this force by being aware of your feelings and instincts, which in turn, will reveal your attachment.

You must trust that your soul knows where and when you need to grow. Trust that your soul knows when it is time to make a change.

For example, you may complain about your job. You may find yourself in a place of unhappiness. Yet you remain attached to the job because you are too frightened to leave your comfort zone. You are afraid to change because it disrupts the false sense of protection derived from your comfort zone. That is stagnation.

Sometimes, life deals you a situation where the job in which you are unhappy is actually taken away from you.

Have you ever noticed that when such a situation befalls

you, it actually ends up being "for the best?" Have you ever recognized retrospectively that such a forced change results in a positive outcome though you were probably highly resistant to it happening?

Your soul is always calling for nourishment. You must create a deeper inner awareness so that you may heed that call confidently and courageously. That is the work you need to do.

How many times have you heard of people who have suffered difficult circumstances or tragedies, but end up living a much more enriched life? Change creates both awareness and understanding of the self as well as offers a dynamic energy for the soul.

Take for example Al Gore, the former Vice President of the United States who lost the presidential election of 2000. That crushing blow in turn became the catalyst for a remarkable transformation of identity. He accepted the loss and embraced the great changes it brought. It led him to the pursuit of his true passion for environmental advocacy. His resulting work in that field garnered him magnificent successes, including a Nobel prize and an Academy Award.

His misfortune and defeat were actually triumphs. Disappointments do not diminish us; rather they are gateways to higher awareness. They can bring us to our soul's purpose.

Remember…

"Every story has an end. But in life every end is just a new beginning."

The next time you lose your job, turn toward the positive. Do not spiral out with the negative because, every change means a new opportunity is potentially out there. The universe may be offering you a chance at a deeper understanding and awareness.

My story…

I remember when I came to understand how the worst things

could also be the best things.

A few years back I decided to travel to Costa Rica. I arrived at the Montreal Airport and handed my ticket to the agent along with my luggage. The agent took one look at my ticket and stopped me in my tracks.

"Sorry sir," she said, "your flight has already departed."

I had mistaken the 10 AM departure time for 10 PM.

I was completely dumbstruck. I remember feeling a surge of anxiety, anger, and panic. But suddenly, with a deep breath, those emotions, threatening eruption, oddly dissipated. They vaporized from my system leaving me with a sudden calmness.

I burst out laughing. It was an odd reaction, and one that surprised even me. The agent gazed at me mystified, and without another word, I simply spun on my heel and walked away.

I remember thinking to myself, "what's next?" I was starting to become sensitive to such experiences and was practicing how to surrender to change, knowing that more often than not it led to new and exciting opportunities that were in my highest interest.

I became wrapped in calmness, and surrendered to the moment relinquishing my intense desire to be in Costa Rica. I knew immediately that this forced change in plans was a sign. The unpredictable had arrived and it altered the course of my destination. I used this moment to observe my thoughts. I stayed aware.

I returned to the ticketing agent and inquired about the next flight to South America.

She told me there was no other flight until tomorrow but there was one leaving for Cancun in two hours.

"I'll take it," I said without hesitation.

When I arrived in Cancun, I hired a taxi to take me to a yoga retreat. I spent two days at the sanctuary, but then was asked to leave because they were fully booked. Again, I embraced the change.

"Can you recommend a secluded retreat?" I inquired.

I was told about a small island off the coast of Cancun with bungalows right on the beach. I embraced the opportunity and dove right into my next unknown adventure.

After four hours of a dusty taxi ride and a two-hour tempestuous boat trip, I arrived on Pelican Island. There were a few kids playing on the beach who greeted me, excited with the newcomer, and offered to help me find the bungalows.

Escorted by the kids, I walked the beach with my bags. As I approached the bungalows, a lady appeared.

"Can I help you?" she asked.

I requested a place to stay. Not having made any arrangements or reservations, I trusted that the universe would take care of me.

"You are indeed very lucky," she beamed, "I have only one bungalow left."

She led me to the bungalow adjacent to a small restaurant nestled on the beach. There, she fetched the key.

"Where are you from?" she inquired.

"Earth," I replied.

That wasn't my normal answer. It just slipped from my mouth. And though I meant it as a joke, as I pressed the word into the air, it suddenly seemed like the best answer—the most unassuming truth.

We shared a smile.

After I settled into the bungalow, I went off to the restaurant for a meal. I caught sight of my host indulging in a salad, and she invited me to join her.

We shared a simple lunch together. Our conversation glided effortlessly and soon shifted into deeper waters as we traded personal histories.

Suddenly her fork fell from her fingers, and tears began to well in her eyes. She buried her face in her hands and allowed her sadness to engulf her. Just as quickly, she wrestled back her composure and in a shy broken voice apologized.

"I'm sorry, I don't know why I am crying in front of you."

I felt the hairs on my skin rise. I knew, at that moment, that this encounter, this woman, her story, being witness to her sorrow, was the unforeseen reason for my detour. I was supposed to be here. The universe guided me to this exact point, place, and time.

I tried to comfort her and tell her all about the twists in my journey that brought me there. I remembered feeling completely secure and solid within, knowing this was meant to be and that by accepting and embracing the uncontrollable changes of the

Forever Now

last several days, I had been preparing for this meeting.

After my host listened to my story with amazement, she told me the full brunt of her devastating circumstances.

"I prayed desperately for help," she shared in a strained voice. "I have not slept a single night here in paradise. I am so confused and depressed beyond anything I have ever experienced."

"Do you think my arrival here is a sign?" I asked.

"I think it means my prayers have been answered," she said with calmness.

She told me that she had been working in a government contracted job for many years, and was appointed to work on a project involving forest conversation and the Native American Indians. She had always wanted this job because of her passion for conserving the environment. She had become concerned about the ecology years ago when she met an Indian seer who told her that humanity is destroying nature, and that it was her purpose in life to use all her political means to restore the environment. As a result, she has put all her heart and soul into the cause.

While she had been on vacation, her co-worker, who also happened to be her closest friend, went behind her back and claimed the project as his own, and gave a final presentation to the board as if he had been the project's sole coordinator all along. My host was shocked, hurt, frustrated, and utterly despondent.

She had needed to go somewhere to try and figure out how to deal with this painful situation. She felt horribly betrayed and was swallowed by deep despair. The despair was paralyzing and she was unsure of her next move. I spent two hours trying to guide her to overcome her emotional entanglements using an emotional release technique that I had studied.

The technique I used required guidance. The participant must be ready to release stressful emotions that block his or her ability to make good decisions. Stressful emotions block clarity

Forever Now

and action. I began by having her observe all of her negative thoughts so she would become aware of her insecurities, angers, resentments, jealousies, and selfish behaviors. Boldness, as I have mentioned, is always the key.

Once blockages dissolves, the natural path toward happiness in all aspects of life becomes apparent. The path becomes illuminated, allowing for the pursuance of long-term love and happiness to become easier.

After I helped my friend through the process, she was overcome by a release of emotions that was supplanted by peace. She hugged me in gratitude, tears running from her eyes. She now felt light and free, and I went to sleep that night knowing that I had achieved a deeper purpose because I allowed myself to be taken on this "accidental" detour.

The next morning, I encountered her at breakfast soaking in her newfound peace and joy.

"Today is the best day of my life," she said.

She inquired how long I would be staying, and I told her that my plans were to leave immediately. She offered me her solemn gratitude as I departed.

I left the island because I knew my purpose for being there had been fulfilled.

From Cancun I made a reservation to go to San Jose, Costa Rica. When I arrived at the airport to check-in for my much anticipated journey to Costa Rica, I was met by some harsh news. My flight was cancelled. Suffice to say, I accepted this news with grace. I once again surrendered to the situation, the universe, and the faith in infinite wisdom.

My life during this period continued with an unpredictable pace and a constant uncertainty of greater purpose. I released myself to the pulse of events beyond my control, and kept keenly aware of my reactions to them.

The next time you miss a plane, train or bus, just relax. Stay aware. Perhaps there is a hidden purpose. Have faith, and perhaps do what I do—shake your head in calm laughter and watch the universe unveil its mystery.

My most difficult experience

Sometimes change can create tremendous upheaval. Following your instincts and having faith in higher awareness and the guiding forces of the universe can be a true test of your temerity. Yet embracing the dynamic shifts that life can present, no matter how arduous, is the only path towards truth and fulfillment.

In 1996, I was traveling from Hawaii with hopes of going to Japan, China, or back to South America. I wasn't sure of which was the appropriate next step to my spiritual journey. I was only armed with the desire to keep seeking and searching, in hopes of better understanding myself as well as my place in the world.

I remember waiting in the Molokai airport for a flight to Honolulu. From there I planned to extend my travels abroad. During the wait, I lost myself in meditation and ended up missing my appointed flight. But by now, I had found a quiet peace by accepting an unpredictable change. I had trained myself to go "with the flow," so to speak.

I took the next flight to Honolulu and met a fellow passenger who inquired about my travel plans. I told her how I wished to visit China, Japan or South America though I hadn't committed my choice as of yet. I was planning to check availabilities once I arrived in Honolulu. A man seated behind me overheard our conversation and suggested that I visit Cambodia. We struck up an intriguing conversation and by the time we reached Honolulu the two of us had built a warm friendship.

He asked me where I was planning to stay that evening, and when I told him I didn't know yet, he graciously invited me to his house. He lived in a magical home, just outside the city, ensconced in the forest area of Manoa. This man had worked in Cambodia as a physician and told me about a woman who had spent much time doing charity work in the country, including what sounded like highly esteemed work with an orphanage.

Forever Now

Several days later I met her. Joanna came over from Kauai with scores of pictures of orphans for which she was trying to find adoptive homes. I truly began to consider her a "Mother Theresa" of sorts. I told her that I would like to work with the children and she invited me to come along with her on her next trip to Cambodia. Her plans for leaving weren't, as of yet, determined. She asked if I could wait.

"Of course!"

I was eager and excited about the opportunity, and was thankful that once again life's unplanned detours seemed to be taking me toward a higher path.

Joanna had a cabin in the Kahili Mountains on Kauai. She let me stay there while she made her preparations for the trip. It was a beautiful, peaceful and isolated sanctuary.

I thought I would be waiting for a couple of days. But those days soon turned into a month. I started to worry. I began to wonder what I had gotten myself into. I remember feeling confused and questioning Joanna's intention. But I soon realized that my negative feelings were rooted in emptiness and fear. I began to use the time to confront these weakening emotions.

Like I have mentioned, our biggest obstacle to change is often our own debilitating emotions. They create a false sense of protection. They keep us in a place of stagnation.

The moment I was able to resolve these emotions, Joanna arrived with the news that she was ready to go to Cambodia. In fact, she had arranged for us to leave the next day. I was finally on my way. I was incredibly thankful because, before even stepping foot in Cambodia, I was already achieving growth.

I arrived full of optimism, but as soon as the plane touched down, my instincts began to question the situation. Joanna had a chauffeur driven Mercedes waiting for her. We were driven to a lavish house, and I quickly began to feel uncomfortable. Her lifestyle did not reflect a person who truly did charity and volunteer work. But rather than judge, I heeded my instincts and requested a modest hotel for my visit.

Forever Now

Again, I'd like to point out how important, if not incredibly imperative, it is to always be in constant awareness of your natural and pure instincts. This is how the soul communicates with the mind. That voice should always be nurtured.

The next day I traveled to the orphanage, but Joanna was nowhere to be found. I encountered a little girl who was very sick. I met the caretaker of the orphanage who everyone called Grandma and inquired after Joanna's whereabouts. No one knew where she was. Grandma explained that Joanna was rarely there. My attention turned back to the girl. Shocked and deeply worried, I made the decision to take her to the hospital where she was diagnosed with internal bleeding. She was admitted in critical condition. I paid for the expenses and immediately went looking for Joanna. I confronted Joanna who told me that many of the children were sick and she did not have the money to pay for their medical care. In fact, she did not have the money to build the orphanage she claimed to be working on.

I was appalled. Joanna had led me to Cambodia on false pretenses. She seemed by all accounts to be a complete fraud.

My anger raged. I could not believe the injustice she was committing. I stormed off and returned to the orphanage where I discovered an even more incredulous horror.

I learned from Grandma that not only wasn't Joanna finding true adoptive homes for these children, she was also buying and selling them. Joanna gave Grandma money to pay mothers a meager sum to give up their children. Joanna would then turnaround and sell these children to western parents or agencies under the ruse of a sanctioned adoption. Joanna had Grandma pay fifty dollars to the Cambodian mothers for their children, and then Joanna in turn would sell the children for thousands.

I confronted Joanna and decided that I would report her to the authorities. But matters began to escalate and reports leaked to the newspapers. NBC and BBC approached me. They wanted me to uncover the story, but soon, I was told by reliable sources that it was no longer safe for me to remain in Cambodia. The reason was simple. The issue of selling children involved prominent politicians and foreign embassies.

Forever Now

I knew I had been brought to Cambodia for a reason. But the decision as to what to do, or how to proceed was a difficult one. I searched within myself trying to determine how I could achieve the most good. I decided that I would indeed leave Cambodia until things cooled off, but I was also going to build that orphanage with my own money.

I took respite in Singapore and made plans for the orphanage's construction. Upon returning to Cambodia, I learned that Grandma had decided to break ties with Joanna. I was tremendously grateful. Grandma and I joined forces and together we built the orphanage. I hired a contractor for the construction and soon the entire village rallied around the cause. Grandma began a textile workshop and began to earn money for the children and the orphanage by creating a cottage industry for making clothes.

By this time, I was spending a lot of time with the people of the village. I learned that the business of buying and selling children was even uglier than I imagined. I found out from my driver that some of the children were being sold for parts, meaning that wealthy parents could buy a child and use that child's body parts in a situation where their own child was in need of an organ donor. It was truly horrific. I investigated further and learned that the organ donor business involved both the Cambodian government and United States Embassy. Corrupt representatives of the United States Embassy were getting part of the money from this black market organ harvesting scheme. How deep and prevalent this nightmare was, I could have only imagined.

I worked hard to create a better environment for these children. We built the orphanage and Grandma created a sustainable business of sewing and textile manufacturing to keep it running. We established a safe and healthy place for the children and a legal means to find them new and loving homes. As I prepared to depart from the village, Grandma wanted to engrave my name in the cornerstone of the orphanage's main house in accordance with Cambodian tradition. But I told her that I would rather see her name there because she was now the sole guardian of those kids. She was their true caretaker and caregiver.

Forever Now

My journey to Cambodia was one of the most emotionally difficult as well as fulfilling experiences of my life. I truly learned that accepting change can lead to immense outcomes, even if it arrives in the smallest and most innocuous manner like it did for me. I embraced the suggestion to visit Cambodia from a stranger I met on a plane trip from Molokai to Honolulu and what resulted was beyond my imagination. The only elements that guided me during that harrowing time were my instincts, awareness, and the purity of the voice within.

Amazing things can indeed happen from the worst of situations. My visit to Cambodia is proof of this.

You must always, no matter how difficult the path, embrace change and surrender your faith to the guiding direction of the universe. Maintain boldness and courage, taking confidence and solace from your true feelings. Those feelings have powerful potential. They create growth and fulfillment as well as lead you toward the opportunity for true happiness.

SPIRITUAL EXERCISE

Make a list of the worst things that have happened in your life so far.

Read over the list. Of the list, choose the event that impacted you most.

Go back and observe the benefits and unexpected outcomes that followed it.

At first you may ask "What benefits?" You may deny that there were any. This response indicates that you have yet to let go of your initial negative impressions of the event. Remember that growth takes time. Look into how the experience filtered into the rest of your life. For example, you may have become more compassionate towards others who experienced a similar situation. You may have become more tolerant in a small way or more generous towards yourself and others. All growth is meaningful. Growth by its very nature can be painful. In order to achieve it, you need to break through your resentment, however subtle, of negative events. You need to penetrate your mind thoroughly in order to reveal the exhilaration of rebirth.

How?

As simple as it may seem, Love is the key. Love has the potency to dissolve negative attachments. True love transcends attachment.

Acknowledge your resentment. Acknowledge the anger and emotions that accompany your experience of the events.

Look into the role you had to play. What role or 'part' did this event force you to play? Be aware of the fact that often we experience being forced into roles that we find uncomfortable.

Stay away from blame as it is a great enemy to growth. Keep the focus on yourself. Ask yourself if reparations need to be made. Saying "I'm sorry" and accepting the role of being the giver of an apology offers a greater sense of freedom.

Be bold!

The best way to solve a problem is to engage it without hesitation.

Begin to practice this wisdom

 **Three**

What Causes Our Downfall?

What causes our downfall?

A few years back, I was in San Francisco sitting with a friend in a café.

We watched as the host was about to seat a couple at the table next to us. The table hadn't been cleared of the glasses from

Forever Now

the previous customers. My friend, who also managed his own restaurant, instinctively knew that no customer would appreciate being seated at a dirty table.

My friend reached over and cleared away the glasses, deftly sliding them over to our table. But when the couple sat down, they made no motion of thanking him for his thoughtful gesture.

That irked him. I could see the disappointment on his face. In fact, not even the host acknowledged the kind deed, even though my friend's act, in some sense, helped the host save face.

By now, my friend was significantly annoyed. He couldn't believe their audacity—neither the customers nor the host expressed the slightest courtesy of a 'thank-you' for his help.

I realized that this minor ruffling of his composure, however slight, was still a very common emotional reaction. When such a situation transpires, where the behavior of others leaves you feeling unappreciated, it all too often creates tension and anger. The irony in this case was that my friend was a man who had been practicing and studying spirituality.

He had attended many lectures, and had amassed an impressive library of books on consciousness evolution. In fact, he had even given talks on philosophy and had become well regarded as a critical thinker in matters of spirituality. But all of this is not to pass judgment on my friend, but more to illustrate the point of how difficult it is to avoid, and overcome the negative feelings of being unappreciated and even disrespected. It was difficult even for my friend, a practicing spiritualist, not to get mired in his own weakening emotions.

I turned to him and asked, "Didn't you see how you just set yourself up for disappointment?"

I explained my logic. I told him that he had imposed his own emotional well-being on the customers and host by expecting appreciation for his favor. Disappointment, if the situation didn't

Forever Now

meet his expectations, was inevitable.

My friend agreed immediately realizing how much control he actually did have over his reaction and ensuing emotions. But he also brought up a critical question.

"I can control my disappointment by managing expectations, but how do I really avoid feeling hurt when such a thing happens?"

I remember how I was just beginning my journey of awakening at that time, and I was very much into observing.

I began wondering what it took to be truly spiritual.

What I started to learn was how important it was to watch thoughts before reacting and how easy it was to fall into the trap of expectations.

I ended up cherishing this exchange with my friend, and felt very grateful for the experience we shared.

Are you attached to your expectations?

Observe how your expectations play a role in eliciting the 'highs and lows' in your life.

Even small expectations, like my friend at dinner, can at first look like insignificant movements of the mind. In fact, such expectations are directly connected to arrogance, and have the power to cause major blockages to your spiritual growth.

Our habit of focusing on the external is a constant source of misfortune and unhappiness. This misappropriated energy can play a big part in the undoing of your daily life. Even at this moment, as you're reading this, you probably have some expectations as to what I might be writing next, or what my point might be.

Due to the ebb and flow of expectations, we often find ourselves constantly dealing with the "highs" and "lows" or the fluctuation of energy levels. This yo-yo pattern causes emotional agitations and blockages to an otherwise calm and vibrant mind.

Our expectations of ourselves and others are often the main sources of discomfort, anxiety, and disappointment.

Observing your expectations among your relationships is a wonderful place to start the process of freeing yourself from debilitating energies. Perhaps you feel you are giving attention to someone who does not return the same level of attention or energy to you. Because of your expectations, you may feel rejected or ignored. This attitude makes it difficult to find a true place of peace let alone love and happiness.

Both the body and the mind suffer from the addiction of "wanting." Wanting always' involves expectations. If you are listening carefully to your body, mind, and soul you can be that much more in tune with what you truly need. And often that will lead to healthy changes instead of enduring the madness of roller coaster emotions that stem from our harmful attachment to expectations.

When you depend on tobacco, drugs, alcohol, food or other attachments, it might at first seem insignificant. However the long term consequences are not only disruptive physically, but they damage your mind and soul. These dependencies prevent you from being in tune with your true needs. Because of that, you will be unable to sense or seek the change you need in order to improve your life. Your path toward love and happiness will become clouded because you have lost clarity. These dependencies prevent you from establishing a deeper awareness of self. Consequently, you cannot achieve your awakening.

What are your choices?

It is your absolute right to experience and do anything you wish. Desires, fantasies, and dreams are all available to you. Learn to approach each of them mindfully. Amazing possibilities are out there awaiting you and ready to be sought.

Try to examine all of your behaviors through your heart. You can learn to change and live differently, guided by your authentic and true voice born from your heart and soul.

Take steps to identify external habits. They prevent us from listening to our hearts. We can identify external habits as those that interfere with our health and progress. External habits are usually clear.

Internal habits, such as *expectation* and *resistance* are more elusive. But they too, must be identified and confronted. Pin-pointing internal habits requires tracing their origin. This requires careful work into the understanding of one's own psychology and personality. This examination will bring you back to your developmental years, but must be done in order for your internal habits to be unraveled, understood and subsequently identified and changed.

It is important to contemplate deeply on patterns of internal and external habits. From there, you can choose to move beyond them. These habits contribute to stagnation and feelings of anxiety and stress.

Accept yourself as the only one responsible for the limitations and blockages that have hampered your forward progress. This is where the practice begins. You should practice being mindful of even the smallest expectations that bubble inside you. Freedom begins when you learn to detach yourself from expectations as well as from trying situations.

When you begin to acknowledge expectations as they arise, you begin to achieve a great clarity. Clarity, as we know, is the initial step towards change. Embracing change is imperative in the process of awakening.

In order to identify your expectations, practice complete awareness. Start feeling how expectations affect your body and temperament. This simple practice has the power to uproot and transform the mind from self-imposed conditioning.

Remember that you alone have the power to make these great changes in behavior. You alone have the power to observe your mind. You alone must bring about the determined focus necessary to detach slowly and propel yourself toward a state of freedom.

Experience has shown me that becoming mindful can and will lead to successes, however small or large. But take care not to let this sense of success interfere with your progress. Success can create a sense of expectation. Strive to reach your goal and successes without the limitations that expectations create. Be wary of adding expectations to your experiences.

SPIRITUAL EXERCISE

What are the things that cause you to struggle and lose focus?

Contemplate on the sources of your blockages. Aim to

practice honesty with yourself. Be honest about the things you dwell on, worry about, and constantly try to control. The only way to truly confront these elements is to be brave enough to tell yourself the truth.

Remember, you are responsible for your own success.

The experience of this practice can unfold unpredictably. Remember, surprise is a great source of joy and inspiration. Allow yourself to be surprised by your own commitment to this goal.

 Four

The Power Of Listening

Kathleen was one of my newest students who arrived for one of my meditation retreats with little previous experience. On the third day of "sitting," she fell into an incredibly blissful state. She expressed overwhelming joy demonstrated by uncontrollable laughter.

Kathleen continued towards this intensely joyous state for the remainder of the retreat, no longer identifying with her previous sense of self or her usual interpretation of the surroundings.

Everyone, fascinated with her state of bliss, began to observe her.

When food was taken away from Kathleen, she expressed very little reaction. She was simply smiling.

Everyone became curious, wanting to know how this blissful state must have felt for her. When asked, she simply said, "I am listening."

When Kathleen walked, she possessed such grace and lightness. Nothing could disturb her. By all indications, she had moved beyond our normal range of experiences.

During meditation, she spoke of hearing brilliant harmonic melodies. When she was in the garden she embraced the trees and rubbed the leaves on her cheeks. She felt compassionately connected and unified with her surroundings. She was at a place where she felt one with the universe.

In her state, she could relate to how brilliant artists, such as Beethoven or Mozart, may have tapped into the source of all creation to compose their extraordinary symphonies.

Kathleen's experience exemplifies one of the stages of awakening. The sounds heard during this blissful state are different from normal hearing. They are not necessarily sounds that come to our ears. They are vibrations that speak directly to the mind, heart, and soul. They are sounds beyond the acoustic. They possess strong emotional elements.

Listening

Listening is the source for all inspiration and creativity. Even looking is a form of listening with the eyes. The process of truly listening is about observing and allowing stimuli to affect not just your senses but your heart.

Forever Now

Can all listen with this capacity? Yes, we can!

We can listen precisely, completely and more mindfully. It takes great patience to learn to listen in the present moment.

Are you listening now?

I once heard about a great sage who advised his students to "listen to the wind." Only years later did I truly grasp the meaning of his wisdom. In order to listen intensely, one has to be acutely living in the present moment. Only then can we access this heightened state of listening.

When you are listening, you are rooted in the "now." When you recognize this and start putting it into practice everyday, you begin to realize how much force and clarity the world can offer you. It is important, therefore, to make every effort to adjust your daily activities and behavior towards developing this new skill of deep listening.

Listening requires practicing mindfulness

Many accidents and misfortunes that we experience are absolutely related to not being in the present moment and not practicing mindfulness. Practicing mindfulness involves speaking and listening with awareness. When we stray from our attentiveness, we make mistakes. Often, we make the same mistakes over and over again. When the mind is absent while we are in action, whether it is taking a walk or some other simple activity, we open ourselves up to adversity.

An old Chinese aphorism best illustrates the point:

A man visited a doctor because of a painful knee injury. The doctor asked him what happened, and the man explained that when he left home, he missed a step, fell down, and bruised his knee. The doctor considered his answer, but suspected there was more to the story.

"No," the doctor said, "I meant, what happened before you

fell down."

"Oh that…" the man replied, "I had a terrible fight with my wife."

The point, of course, is that the man was not living in the present moment. Misfortune found him the moment his attention was compromised.

After treating the man's injury, the doctor sent him home with an advice:

"The next time you have an argument, be mindful enough to reduce the internal agitation before engaging in any activity."

Most of our accidents are the result of distractions. Daily practice of mindfulness is the solution.

Listening is a natural skill of the soul.

Every song, movie, book, and magazine has a message for you. Every place you visit and every one you meet has a message for you. Not only is there a message, but the message is reflective of your own melody. There is a unique harmony between you and your world if you listen.

When you practice how to listen deeply, you will start to recognize synchronicities. These synchronicities can occur in the form of signs. Signs are among the ways the universe uses to communicate with you and guide you.

When you see or feel a sign, take it as a reminder to listen even deeper. As you listen you move towards a more blissful state. Do not hesitate at the subtle transformation in your state of being. Remember, hesitation is a form of fear and stagnation.

Take time to contemplate and grasp your situation. For example, contemplate on the last sentence. Sit with it. Absorb it. Understand it. The feeling of grasping something is satisfying in a calm way. It is a knowingness in your heart—an inner silence that allows you to hear and know beyond your current capacity. This is intuition.

Understanding Intuition

When confronted with any situation, no matter how intricate, the first thought that enters your mind is intuitive. Many people don't hear this first thought. It has become lost in the din of other thoughts and emotions. The only way to recognize this first thought is by carefully listening for it.

You cannot hear a whisper in a loud room. Similarly, you will not hear the first thought of intuition in a loud mind.

Be careful not to get confused and mired in other people's thoughts, responses, and influences. Put trust in your own feelings and your hearing.

Your first thought is powerful and penetrating. Be careful not to contaminate its potency with the influence of your second thought or other people's thoughts.

Deep listening creates a transformation that brings you beyond the confusion of outside concerns and opinions.

Use this method of listening as you follow this text. Read as if you are listening. Allow your thoughts to freely arise in response to these words. Observe the thoughts.

Listen, and let go.

Harnessing this intense passion for listening will give you great power to make changes in your life and to your behavior. Remember, change is the key to awakening. Recognizing and embracing change is nourishing for the soul. The power to listen enables this process. Listening facilitates change.

Now listening becomes rapture.

Through listening, you will begin to observe how you and

other people carry around worries and expectations. Listening allows you to become a more acute observer.

As you listen more, your desire for this practice will also exponentially rise. Listening will embolden your inner awareness. This realization will make you bolder.

The practice of listening allows you to approach a powerful state of peace and bliss. This state is available to you all the time. The reason it often escapes our grasp is that we are undermined by our distractions and expectations. Freeing ourselves from distractions and expectations, and committing to intense listening will transform our perspective.

Take for example those students who have the remarkable ability to get good grades in school while seemingly doing little work. They whiz through exams while other students plod, working as hard as they can only to achieve mediocre results.

The difference between the two categories of students is in

their ability to listen deeply. Deep listening allows for a deeper saturation of information.

Deep listening helps us access our memory.

You can practice developing your listening skills through small steps. Begin, for example, by paying closer attention to your favorite kind of music.

In time, as your practice develops, you will become aware of the rhythms of your entire body, including an acute awareness of your skin, your eyes, and every cell within. When you are able to listen deeply to your body, you are able to access a whole extended realm of intelligence and information. Our intellect does not reside only in the brain.

Listening also has the power to further awaken intuition when you practice focusing on the solar plexus region (Spiritual heart) during meditation.

Intuition is the fusion of the higher mind and heart. It is the harmony between the thinking mind and the feeling heart. Intuition comes prior to feeling, and feeling is the communication between the soul and the body.

What is intuition and how can you see it in your daily life?

- Every time you have an idea, the first thought is the purest. Isolate it and act upon it.

- The second thought is less clear. Ignore it. More often than not, it contains aspects of criticisms and expectation.

- The thoughts after that are even further contaminated and manipulated by the mind.

- The worst approach is seeking another person's opinion.

Learn to rely and act upon your first thought. Go forward

emboldened with its full force. Do not pay attention to doubt or hesitation. Remember, listening is a prerequisite to intuitive feeling.

What is the purpose of feeling?

The purpose of feeling is to deliver experience. Feeling also delivers warnings about choices. These are the soul's messengers.

What is the soul?

The soul is that part of the creator that all of us possesses within us.

True listening is silence, and silence is the song of the soul. Great art and creativity is not created under pressure. There is a sense of freedom in creativity.

To cultivate your inner joy, you must first befriend yourself by beginning these aforementioned practices.

Listening deeply allows you to access and reap the awards of inner happiness. This inner happiness has enough power to attract anyone and anything into your life. Listening offers you the chance to access and experience the fulfillment of your desires.

SPIRITUAL EXERCISE
Nindera Meditation

Nindera helps you develop intuition.

Lie down flat on your back.

Cover yourself with a blanket if you need to keep warm. Being comfortable and relaxed is essential.

Spread your arms face up by your side.

Put your focus on the spiritual heart, which like I have mentioned is the solar plexus.

Inhale on a count of five.

Exhale as you count to five.

Continue doing this for ten minutes, focusing your attention on feeling your spine opposite your solar plexus. Keep each inhalation focused on that sensation.

Continue with the same pace and visualize the ocean water rushing to shore with your inhalation and then receding with each exhalation. Focus on visualizing the details of the experience—the wave, the sand, and the bubbles. Continue this practice for ten minutes.

This exercise leads to calmness, peaceful joy, and a blissful state. It has the power to help you develop compassion, and, of course, intuition. It's important to practice this meditation every day, at least once per day, for at least twenty minutes.

 **Five**

The Art Of Surrender

I used to live in large city in Canada where I owned three successful restaurants in a bustling district along one of the most coveted blocks of real estate.

The restaurants were always jam-packed. I loved the ambiance, the scrumptious food, great décor, and abundant energy. The atmosphere was tremendously festive. Even the couples waiting in line for a table would be smiling.

Forever Now

I could feel the love emanating from every one—the cook, the hostesses, and the clients.

One evening, buoyant and so alive with the evening's energy, I roamed the room dressed in a knockout Italian suit overseeing the activities at the restaurant and greeting the customers, many of whom I knew by name.

I remember stepping outside into the crisp air, overcome with gratitude. But there, I stumbled upon a drunken old beggar who had made camp on the steps next to the entrance of my restaurant.

I paused. The sight was so very incongruous with the elegance and affluence that surrounded me and which reflected who I was to the world.

Suddenly, something inside my heart made a switch. I took a turn and found myself embracing the art of surrender.

Instead of judging this homeless man, I went back inside, grabbed two beers from the bar, and joined him right on the stairs before my own restaurant.

I was overcome with the need to connect with this man on a human level. I wanted to experience his life perspective. I wanted to be on the same vista as this down-trodden impoverished man, who I could see, by the look on the face of every passerby, was being judged for his mere existence.

We sat quietly sipping our beers; then I extended my hand, pretending to be a beggar, and started asking people for money. I was assaulted by the disgust on their disapproving faces. I felt first hand what it was like to be slapped by the cold force of rejection.

I had never in my life ever felt a sense of disgrace—the sense of floating in exile—the sense of being homeless, unwanted, and disrespected. I was profoundly humbled by this new awareness.

"Why do you drink?" I asked the man.

"To forget everything," he whispered.

The brutality of his response hit me hard.

His condition affected me so much that I continued giving him money for weeks thereafter, much to the chagrin of the community. Fellow business owners criticized me. Accusations followed. Apparently, people thought I was enabling this homeless man—encouraging him to drink more.

I have to admit that I too had once shared this philosophy of "the enabler," but my switch in perspective was leading me down the path of surrendering. I had arrived at a juncture of self-realization. Perhaps it was I and the pious judgmental community of successful business owners, that had created the social misfortune and viability of a drunk and homeless man.

I realized at that moment how we all need to surrender to

the reality of what people are rather than impose our rules upon them like a barb of imprisonment.

You cannot contain or subjugate another person with your predetermined conjuring of what you believe they should be.

When you embark on this trajectory of judgment, you have not surrendered to yourself.

Sitting on the steps that evening, with a beer in hand, I surrendered myself to this other human's lifestyle, which included drinking and soliciting strangers for help and money.

Why shouldn't I accept him?

Within the act of acceptance, is an act of life. I acknowledged, accepted, and surrendered to the fact that this homeless man had chosen his own experience of life.

I knew that was not all of who he was. What I witnessed and

Forever Now

experienced alongside him was merely a part of his story. It was a part of his history, but not his mystery. He, like all of us, had more to live, and discover.

History—Not Mystery.

One morning, I placed a blanket around him. Soon thereafter, he disappeared. Weeks passed and I didn't see him. He didn't come back to the steps, and I never saw him around the neighborhood. I remembered wondering what had happened to him, and if he was okay.

After a month or so, as I headed to the restaurant to greet the busy weekend crowd, I was approached by the beggar. But this time, I didn't recognize him at all.

He stood before me, tall and dignified. His hair was cut. He was clean-shaven and well dressed.

We took a seat in our familiar spot—the concrete steps.

I was completely floored. I couldn't believe his transformation.

"I went home," he began to say, "and I saw my family for the first time in many years. I discovered that they still love me. I couldn't believe their love."

"You know," he continued, "when you sat next to me on those stairs, and we drank together, you showed me love. You accepted me for who I was. In a way, your kindness sparked my change. It gave me the courage to seek out my own family. It made me realize that the only person who stopped loving me—was me."

He smiled. His face beamed with the pure light of life.

"And now I have a job."

I was overcome with emotion. Warmth filled my heart. I felt honored and privileged to have played a hand in reawakening the spirit that was lying dormant within this man.

I shared my experience of surrendering with him. I told him how I had released myself from feelings of judgment and disapproval and saw him as just another man within a common world. I extended my "secret of self love."

The lesson we both shared was this:

Be present in the now.

Surrender yourself.

Love others for who they are and not for who you want or expect them to be.

We are all perfect just the way we are.

We must love ourselves for who we are.

The art of surrendering means to listen to the voice of your soul. It is your true identity and it will guide you to your true destiny.

Once you begin practicing the art of surrendering, you will notice that your creativity will multiply. Your goals, desires, and dreams will become more accessible. Possibilities will come into grasp.

Surrendering in the present moment is the best preparation for the future. No matter what the future holds, the most important thing is to LIVE RIGHT HERE IN THE NOW.

Surrendering and living in the moment are the foundation for the concept of "Forever Now," which is a fusion of the past, present, and future. Seize the secret of surrendering the present, and the future will unfold effortlessly.

Surrendering does not mean giving up or accepting defeat. This is an essential element to remember. On the contrary,

Forever Now

surrendering fuels you with the power and freedom to be. It simply means letting go.

When we are in the mental frame of surrendering, we are filled with gratitude for every relationship that enters our lives. Expectations are put aside when the act of surrendering becomes our full focus. This is an essential ingredient for awakening because surrendering helps us remain mindful and present.

Remember, we are connected to a great source of energy and are gifted with unlimited possibilities. This greatness is always present.

When you surrender, all barriers and obstacles recede and you can better connect with that great energy and open yourself to infinite possibilities.

Unconditional love

Happiness never left you. You left happiness.

There is no love greater than unconditional love for it gives without asking anything in return.

In the arms of unconditional love, physical beauty, intelligence, and abundance envelop you.

In your life, when hardship replaces happiness, more often than not, it was you who left happiness. This happened because you were distracted and you rejected the present moment.

Happiness never left you. It is forever available to you. It is always within reach.

Remember my stories regarding Cancun, Costa Rica, and Cambodia? My act of surrendering and embracing uncertainty led me not only to happiness, but also to my true purpose.

The road need not be linear.

Your purpose is exactly what you are doing and thinking

now. Do not focus your energy and attention in the realm of a far-away future. Do not become consumed by events, no matter how imposing, that haven't taken place yet. Love being in the now.

Perhaps there have been days when you felt like everything was going against you.

This is simply never true.

More than likely, it was your stubbornness, resistance, and hostility that had created the hardship. Your condition will continue as such until you stop fighting, and surrender.

Do not expect someone else to bring you happiness or change your situation.

Your happiness is directly proportional to your ability to surrender. When you surrender, you will find that situations of stress and conflict will gracefully resolve themselves.

When you practice the act of surrendering with pure awareness, devoid of blame and regrets, life will begin to fall into place.

SPIRITUAL EXERCISE
The HU mantra

The HU spiritual exercise helps you expand your capacity to give and receive love. It will also help you develop greater compassion, as well as increase your intuition.

The HU, pronounced hue, is an ancient word for Sacred. It has been called a love song to the Sacred because of its capacity to open the heart to unconditional love. By singing or chanting the word "HU," you are calling on Divine Spirit with this intention:

"Not my will, but, May Thy Will be Done!"

Forever Now

Chanting the HU is a practice of surrendering, as well as expanding your capacity to give and receive love.

This mantra can be used by anyone regardless of his or her spiritual path. The HU is to be sung once or twice a day for fifteen to twenty minutes, preferably upon waking in the morning, and before retiring at night.

Find a quiet place. Lie down, or sit with your back straight, your feet planted on the floor, and your hands resting comfortably in your lap. Sitting is recommended over lying down as the latter can often lead to an unplanned nap.

Recall an incident that brought love or happiness to your heart. Perhaps think about someone, a pet, or something you love. This is done simply to open your heart to love.

With your heart filled with love, put your focus at the point between your eyebrows, often referred to as the spiritual eye, third eye or tisra til.

In a long, drawn out breath, sing the word HU-U-U-U.

Sing this song either silently or softly in prayer during mediation sessions.

The HU can also be used when you find yourself in situations where you need more insight, rejuvenation, or protection. Your aim is to connect with the light and sound current of the ultimate reality—also referred to as the vibrations of the Pure Essence.

 **Six**

The Secret Of Self-Love

Every creature seeks wholesomeness through love.

You can only assume the journey of seeking and achieving self-love by adopting self-inquiry and self-understanding. They are at the root of self-love. Love what you have become.

Love all. However, in order to love others truthfully, you

Forever Now

must first love what you have become.

In order to save someone else, you must first save yourself.

The practice of self-love asks that you pray for yourself first.

Recall the safety announcement we commonly hear on airplanes: "In case of emergency, secure the oxygen mask tightly around your mouth before helping others."

It is important to send gratitude toward yourself first. From there, your love can extend.

Give yourself prosperity.

When we say a prayer at a Thanksgiving dinner, allow that prayer to also be for you.

No one is in need of prayer more than you.

You may ask, "Does the Sacred need my prayers?"

On the contrary, the Sacred prays for you.

Self-love means being truthful with yourself but it doesn't mean being hard on yourself. It is important to liberate yourself from past mistakes and lost opportunities. The past is dead. Only the present is alive. The future is not born yet.

Observe and Examine

You have probably already realized that being hard on yourself never benefits you in the present. The absence of self-love fosters stress, unhappiness, and insecurity.

In fact, our physical state is very much linked to our attention on self-love. Turmoil of negative emotion affects one's heart rate, breathing, and blood pressure. This physical intensity causes further biological agitation, which can lead to greater health complications including the destruction of cells in your nervous system. These cells are not regenerative. Once lost, they can never be replaced.

Stress

On the most basic level, physical agitation leads to a loss of energy. Energy, as we well know, is a vital element in sustaining life. The diminished cells contain crucial amounts of energy that are no longer available to the body.

Stress not only disrupts your awareness, but also has other physical effects. You age quicker: Your hair turns gray and wrinkles appear on your face. If the negative emotions persist, they can eventually cause psychological damage and a loss of sense.

These scientific facts need to be considered. And once physical damage occurs, it is difficult, or, in some cases, impossible to reverse.

The internal and external effects that stress has on your body are compounded by the fact that such a negative state of living causes you to emit a negative vibration into the universe.

This vibration arrives in the form of anger and its consequence manifests itself according to "the law of attraction." That law is based upon the tenet that what you think about, you bring about. Therefore, unhappiness can beget even more unhappiness. Anger begets more anger.

You may be familiar with these common adages: "Angry people live in an angry world;" or "When you are angry, you feel stuck and there is no way out."

Let me remind you that there is, indeed, a way out. Meditation, Tai-Chi, yoga, jogging, or simply taking a walk, are valid methods that can give you release. These practices help improve your level of tolerance and provide you with a way out. They bring clarity and help you return to the present moment.

Consider the ancient proverb:

"Curse those who curse the other and bless those who bless the other."

SPIRITUAL EXERCISE

The next time you are cursing someone with your words know that you are also cursing yourself. Conversely, when you bless someone with your words, thoughts, or actions, you are also blessing yourself.

The next time you start acting from a place of agitation and anger, stop yourself! How does it benefit you? Can you honestly provide a positive answer?

Practice self-love with awareness. When you do, you will begin to feel the transformative power of love. Your self-worth and health will improve.

The practice of self-love and awareness is a lifelong commitment. It is a journey akin to fate—revealing itself only when you are ready for it.

Seize the words on these pages.

Apply them.

Contemplate…

I promise they will revisit you when you least expect them to.

 **Seven**

The Ego

Your worst enemy is your mind… until you make it your friend.

A beautiful mind is one which is no longer controlled by the Ego. Though the Ego will remain present, its original power will be diminished.

Envision your mind as your bedroom, and your Ego as the light. Since the power of the Ego has already been diminished, you are the only one that can control it. A beautiful mind is a room that contains a light bulb but the light bulb is not on. You can choose whether or not to turn on the light bulb, but the light bulb no longer turns on of its own volition.

Achieving full presence means that you can elect to turn on emotions such as jealousy, fear, or sadness, if you so desire, but these emotions no longer rule you.

A dwarf masquerading as a giant.

The Ego is often presented as a giant in most spiritual literature. In fact, Freud dedicated a large part of his life's work to uncovering the Ego. But the truth is that the Ego is a dwarf.

The Ego is actually a branch of the lower mind. Because it is constantly striving to shine, it assumes the cloak of intelligence.

The Ego is what stops us from self-love. It is often our biggest impediment. The Ego manifests itself in many forms, and can be discerned in every hostile situation.

For these reasons, it is important to detect and isolate the Ego with your heightened awareness.

The purpose of the Ego is to distract and disconnect the body from the mind. The Ego makes the body and mind opaque from the soul.

This is what establishes the Ego as a master of disguise. Often when you are hurt or offended, the ensuing negative emotions are a product of the Ego. They reflect your identification with the Ego.

Imagine yourself in a laboratory where you can observe and reenact your reactions toward people. Carry this laboratory metaphor with you every time you meet someone. Whenever you are involved in a relationship, simply and calmly observe your reactions.

There is old Native American tale that illustrates the idea of the Ego.

A captured man beseeched the tribal chief for his freedom. The chief took a deep look into the man's eyes and prophesized: "There are two dogs inside you. These two dogs are in conflict with each other. One dog is good and the other dog is evil. Now tell me which one is going to win?"

The man quietly answered, "The one I feed the most."

When you are in conflict with yourself, who do you feed the most? Your true self or your Ego?

Not long ago, I considered the Ego my enemy, and in time, I realized that even the Ego has its purpose. It accomplishes its job very well. That is why we often find ourselves consumed in chaos and confusion.

The Ego as automaton

Self-centered rumination is the influence of the Ego in its natural form. In this state, you are operating in an automatic mode, under the command of your Ego. You are put into a defensive position, and in the process of defending yourself, you are predisposed to generating a muddled and chaotic state.

A true story:

Allow me to share a very tragic and horrifying incident involving a young family.

This couple and their young son were returning home from a party late one evening. As they entered their apartment, their small dog scampered up with its tail wagging.

The husband accidentally stepped on the dog's tail. The dog immediately yelped, and the wife scooped the pet into her arms.

She glared at her husband with fierce resentment, "Why did you step on the dog?"

"I didn't mean to," he defended himself. "He was just in my way."

"Don't lie," she snapped at him, "it's not like this is the first time."

The conflict escalated. Soon the husband and wife were hurtling venomous insults at each other.

Suddenly the wife dashed into the kitchen in a fury. She blindly seized a kitchen knife, and attacked her husband in apoplectic rage. She stabbed him repeatedly.

The husband dropped to the floor in a bloodied heap.

She continued stabbing him.

Their ten-year-old son stood frozen—a witness to the entire horror.

I know about this story because the neighbors had summoned me to the scene. At the time, I was living in Iran working as the Counsel On Duty for foreign families.

I was one of the first to arrive on the scene. I remember the details with crystal clarity. The wife was cleaning the floor in ghostly shock. The husband lay gurgling on the floor. And the boy stood eight to ten feet away—a complete zombie lost within the recesses of his consciousness.

I notified the police at once, and requested an ambulance. The husband died on the way to the hospital.

In the end, the wife was taken to prison, and the boy was ushered off to live with his uncle.

I bring up this story to remind us of the many times we have overreacted. Think back to moments in your life where you erupted during a situation, that when examined later, seemed incredibly insignificant. Often these are moments entwined with the lower mind—the Ego.

With the passage of time, you once again reconnect with the higher mind. When this happens, you gain new perspective and are suddenly aware of how you could have behaved differently.

I didn't know any better!

One way to let go of the regrets and self-condemnation that often accompanies self-disapproval and disappointment is to be honest with yourself about your conduct. Being honest means telling yourself the reason you behaved as you did. When you get to the core of the matter, the truth is:

You did not know any better.

You can repeat to yourself: "I fell into anger (or any other emotion) because I did not know any better. Otherwise I would have behaved differently."

On the surface, the above reason may seem childish. But when you really think about it, you will realize that if you knew better, you would not have done what you later regretted. You may argue that you knew better but did it anyway for some reason. This in itself clearly shows you didn't know any better or you would have done the right thing!

Now when you are assaulted by old feelings such as blame, hurt, and anger just tell yourself that you didn't know any better. When you do this, you'll be surprised that your mind will become quiet. That voice in your head that keeps reminding you about everything you've done wrong will suddenly shut up the moment you admit that you didn't know any better. Try it.

Start communicating with your higher mind.

Forever Now

When you observe with clarity, blame and guilt are immediately removed from your thoughts. This allows your inner awareness to deepen. You begin to know yourself better and discover the freedom that comes with a lighter attitude toward difficulties, conflict, and hurt.

I remember the deep resentment I had toward my parents for a long time. Years later, as I awakened, I realized they really did not know any better.

The power of that realization was immense, yet the realization itself was so very simple. I instantly surrendered many years of hurt and resentment. I vanquished myself of the pain that had been haunting me for years.

This epiphany brought me tremendous clarity. I worked through my emotions and consciously traced the dynamics of our past relationship. I became aware of my own guilt and blame, confronted my Ego, and let go.

Whenever I feel offense today, I am able to acknowledge the influence of the Ego through the practice of watching and observing.

Anger and resentment are negative emotions inextricably tied to the Ego. For many people, these negative emotions are very familiar. In fact, they are so habitual they have become nurturing emotions.

It is difficult for many of us to relinquish our grip on these emotions because of the false sense of protection they provide. Anger gives us an illusionary sense of justice—that of being right. But more often than not, it makes us miserable.

You are most unhappy when you cling tenaciously to the Ego—to anger and resentment. This misery perpetuates itself until you carefully observe your thoughts and take great heed to watch your every reaction.

Without adopting this vigilant observation of self, your mind will be a battlefield.

A New Stage of Evolution

When you designate certain people as your enemy because they ignore you or don't offer you as much attention and respect as you feel you deserve, you are operating from the lower mind.

The lower mind influences you to have a negative attitude towards individuals you resent. It coaxes you into carrying negative narratives with you so that you can try to recruit others to side with you—to help prove you right.

You do not need the comfort of such confirmation. You are beyond the manipulations of the lower mind. Remember, you are enmeshed in the business of spirituality.

Now is the time for you to start living a happier and healthier life. If it's not now, when? You need to become aware of what prevents you from experiencing the highest state of being. It is time to emerge from the cocoon and learn to see your selfishness, fear, and jealousy projected against those whom you reject.

Unchecked, these ruthless acts and reactions lead to the "Law of Cause and Effect" variably known as "The Laws of Attraction," and "Karma."

Move to the next higher level of thought by quieting your mind and opening your heart. Open your heart to those who acknowledge and love you as well as to those who do not acknowledge and love you.

If you love only those who love you, how will you be authentically rewarded? How will you grow?

SPIRITUAL EXERCISE

Now that you are practicing being the observer, you have entered into the realm of The Practitioner. You are now ready to live in the NOW.

Recognize there is plenty of love in your heart to gift to others and much more left over to nourish yourself. So give love freely, and be open to receive without expectation.

Choose this experience to be your practice. It is the key to achieving authentic happiness, love and freedom.

 **Eight**

The Mysterious Coin:
Don't Take It Personally

Here is a true story about a friend of mine, who had worked till dawn to complete his art project. It was the completion of a demanding project that took a total of seventeen days. Full of excitement and relief, he took an early morning stroll to get a cup of coffee from a local coffee shop. It was a cold winter morning.

On his way, he noticed a stranger approaching and in his jolly mood, smiled broadly and greeted the stranger a good morning. The next thing he remembered was struggling to get up from the ground. The stranger had punched him on the face and knocked him down.

Gazing into the cold eyes of his assailant who was standing over him, he asked with a confused facial expression, "Why did you hit me when all I did was say 'Good morning' to you?" The stranger said nothing—he just stared, shaking in anger. Not knowing what else to do or say to his attacker, my friend explained to the stranger that he was on his way to get a cup of coffee, and asked the stranger to join him. Again, the stranger just stared at him. As a painter, my friend was a sensitive man and could feel the emotional burden of his attacker. As he got up from the ground, he said to his attacker, "Come on, let's go. You'll feel much better after a cup of hot coffee." The stranger just stood there still shaking in anger. But as my friend started walking away to the coffee shop, the stranger followed him.

When they got to the coffee shop, my friend got a table for

two and ordered two cups of coffee. As they sat there for a while, face to face, drinking coffee in silence, my friend looked at the stranger compassionately and questioned him once again why he decided to hit him so early in the morning, just for saying "Good morning."

In a trembling, low tone and sad voice, the stranger began to speak for the first time and my friend listened absorbedly. "I have not had any sleep because I have been walking around all night in the cold. When I saw your smiling face, it really made me mad. That's why I hit you. I am sorry." Giving the response sufficient time to settle, my friend patiently queried, "Is that all?"

Clinching his cup of coffee in both hands, the stranger cleared his throat, looked down on the table and began to speak again in low tone. "When I got home from work yesterday, I was really looking forward to seeing my wife and sharing a pleasant evening with her. Instead I walked in and caught her sleeping with another man in our bed. I was so shocked that I didn't know what to do. I turned around and walked out of the house and I have been walking around ever since until I saw you."

There was a long silence as both men considered the news. "Well, I know of a story very similar to yours, but it had a slightly different ending," my friend said.

A man that I know quite well came home one day and found his wife in bed with another man. He walked closer and stood by the side of the bed, looking at his wife and her lover. There was tremendous tension in the air. The man felt let down, yet, in a detached tone, said to his wife's lover, "You can go. But before you go, I would like you to pay for my wife's service to you." In a state of fear and panic, the fellow reached into the pocket of the trouser that he was hurrying to put on, emptied all the cash and handed it over to the woman's husband. The husband took only one coin from the stash and handed the rest of the money back. The fellow took the stash and quickly ran out of the house shaking in fear and confusion.

Holding up the coin, the man turned to his wife and said, "Starting today, this coin will be placed on the dining room table and should never be removed. But if you have any problem with that, you can pack your things and leave permanently."

"For the past seventeen years, I had stared at that coin on our dining room table and wondered why it was so sacred," my friend said, looking at his attacker with a strange smile. "My parents never said a word about it. I just knew it was never to be removed. Even when we had guests at the house, any questions about the coin was met with a silent stare. Gradually, our friends learned to simply ignore the coin. It was shortly before my mother passed away last year that she told me the story behind the mysterious coin. Until today, I never told this story to anyone."

The two men finished their coffee, and with fresh insights, went their separate ways.

SPIRITUAL EXERCISE

Just put the book down at this point and go into silence. Continue with the next chapter after your contemplation.

 **Nine**

Forever Now: Savor the Present

Most people are not actually living in the present. When you embrace the now, there is a marked difference in your quality of being.

When you live in the now, your actions and behavior demonstrate obvious signs.

Daily, I witness people around me—educated individuals—claiming to be living in the present moment, but, in truth, they are not.

Forever Now

These individuals, who believe they are "living in the moment" still pass judgment, exhibit anger, make assumptions, and routinely engage in conflict. They raise their voices when they can reap the benefits.

You cannot just claim or speak about living in the moment. You must exhibit the action.

Ask yourself, why is it so difficult to be simple?

When you are actually rooted in the present moment, it is difficult to say anything to hurt anyone or make mistakes.

Forever Now means seeking the path towards living in the present moment.

Observing sweet, sweet breath

Let us begin with breath observation. Follow your breath in and out. Observe your inhalations and exhalations until your air becomes crisp and sweet.

When you observe your breath over a period of time, you are met with strong feelings of tranquility and joy.

Using the practice of "touch" is another way of claiming the idea of *Forever Now*. Every time you touch, even the most ordinary or mundane object, do it mindfully. Touch the handle of a door with intention and focus. Observe how it feels as well as how it makes you feel.

By immersing yourself in the practice of "now," you will begin to feel a great peace. A child-like playfulness will return to your life.

What is more delicious than kissing your lover on the lips, and feeling the warm energy of love?

You must choose to become aware of the benefits of practicing *Forever Now*. Either you will remain in a state where your emotions dictate heightened reactions or you will seek a more solid ground of clarity, tranquility, and joy.

The choice is yours.

Forever Now

Every time you face complexity, examine your reactions. Make this your daily practice. *Forever Now* exists through your choices.

Remember, you have the power to choose either a chaotic landscape or one of calmness and beauty. Trust your instincts, feelings, vision, mission, and purpose.

Determining the direction of your life is within your grasp.

Humans are distinct from plants, elements, and animals in their conscious choice of freedom.

We are subjected to various sets of universal laws that we cannot fight.

The Law of Gravity is one such example. If you climb a tree and let go of the branch that supports you, you will plummet.

But, there are also laws you can disobey. Depending on your choices, the outcome will vary radically. One of these laws is the Law of Cause and Effect.

The sole outcome of your destiny is determined by your daily choices.

Remember, your present condition is nothing more than the crystallization of your past activities.

The Recipe of Choice

Always observe what you are choosing. Be aware and observe.

You are an infinite being with infinite possibilities. Don't choose to limit yourself because of the old patterns of your mind.

It may seem difficult to act on a thought that destabilizes your life. But remember, thoughts that offer change are actually bringing your life back into true balance. That is how you truly start living the life of Forever Now.

Forever Now

Make a list of your dreams and inspirations.

Write down your first goal—that long ago dream you desired.

You cannot achieve balance if you do not attain clarity. Work towards knowing yourself.

We are blessed to live in a time when great advances abound. There are no physical, mental, or social limitations that obstruct us from living according to the practice of *Forever Now*.

Try and draw inspiration from the many individuals who have conquered perceived limitations and proceeded to accomplish great things.

Consider individuals like Terry Fox who glided solo across Canada with artificial limbs. Individuals like him are inspired with great clarity. Nothing stops them.

Make sure your scripted goals and purpose align with your authentic self.

Organize and plan your day embracing the choices that will

keep you focused and enable you to reach your goals. This will ensure that your life flows with purpose and you don't become distracted. When ambiguous and trying situations arise, you will be more cognizant of your direction because of your determined choice to stay focused on your goals.

Your distractions and chaos will lessen as you remain steadfast on your journey to preserving and meeting definite goals.

You will soon notice that the people around you will become calmer because they will be inspired by your clarity and determination.

Obstacles will still always appear. Life does not go away. But do not be daunted. You are transcending to higher levels of your self. Remember, you never stop growing.

Life does not go away

Extraordinary life

When you truly begin to honor and love yourself, life becomes extraordinary. What you bestow upon yourself, you will also see in the world around you. That same level of love and honor will return to you through your surroundings.

Take small and determined steps toward your goals so as to not get overwhelmed. Goals are more accessible in palatable chunks. You must always be able to visualize yourself moving toward your achievements.

Remember to reward yourself for accomplishments. Refine your life—offer more love and quality to your life and to the world around you.

SPIRITUAL EXERCISE
SELF-CARE

Rewarding yourself and meeting the essence of self-care can be very simple:

- Light fragrant candles accompanied by a refreshing long bath
- Take a walk in nature
- Read a great book to someone you love
- Listen to beautiful music
- Dance, dance, dance
- Give and receive hugs
- Practice yoga and stretching
- Get a massage

- Compose a beautiful note
- Help someone unexpectedly

I have discovered that when I write a Thank You letter or do something thoughtful for someone, my goals and dreams are stimulated. Loving thoughts infuse me with abundant energy. I am uplifted throughout my day.

Living Forever Now

Forever Now is a simple life concept. Though it requires daily and constant practice, it is an authentic and pure way of living. At first, it may take a great amount of focus to achieve this way of living, but in time your deliberate attention will become second nature. You will begin to flow down the path of *Forever Now* effortlessly. Just like any new set of skills, the more you practice them, the more they will become ingrained into your natural self.

With practice, your attitude and actions will shift, at first incrementally, but in time more comprehensively. It is always difficult to change patterns. It requires constant effort until the new skills and tools become gracefully assimilated into your daily living. But in the end, a resolute tranquility will nourish your

Forever Now

internal state while externally, an arena of infinite possibilities will become within reach.

Forever Now is a simple, yet truthful path toward happiness and fulfillment.

Remember, it all begins with hearing your soul's voice. Listen and observe your feelings as well as your surroundings. Be deliberate. Become more aware. Learn to focus on your instincts.

Separate yourself from your negative and debilitating emotions.

Your instincts and your feelings guide you towards your truth. They are your internal compass alerting you of situations and relationships that suppress your souls' spirit.

Heed this voice.

Embrace the changes your soul requires.

Often our instincts and feelings tell us when we need to seek change in order to realign ourselves with who we truly are.

Permitting these feelings to blossom and allowing for the changes they beckon lead to authentic happiness. But often, we shun change because of the anxiety it creates inside us.

Remember, stagnation is another form of fear. Fear keeps us imprisoned.

Your spirit craves change. That is how you grow. That is how you become more aware.

Listening to your instincts and feelings—your soul's voice—is how you are innately guided towards making the necessary changes you need for greater unfoldment. Change is how we nourish our soul. The negative feelings that prevent us from welcoming change are our illusionary protective emotions. Overcome your anger, fear, anxiety, and resentment.

Push yourself out of your comfort zone.

Awakening is not always comfortable. In fact, it can be very painful. But trust that the changes you strive for are leading you towards a much more fulfilled existence. As you become more confident in the practice of observing, and staying aware, you will gain more courage in bearing the turmoil of change.

Forever Now

Soon, the negative emotions that previously prevented you from surrendering to change and thwarted your progress will diminish. With practice, you will be able to recognize your fear, and anger, and know that those emotions do not lead you toward your productive goals. Consequently, you will dismiss them with ease, whereas in the past you would have clung to them for security.

Trust that the universe is synchronized with your true emotions.

Surrender to unforeseen detours in life. When you become open to your intuition, you will be able to recognize your true wants and your needs. You are then able to embrace life's forced changes, knowing that they may lead you to your ultimate fulfillment.

Take a deep breath. Surrender.

Surrendering means freedom. And freedom affords you great joy and happiness.

Forever Now is about living completely in the present moment. Be constantly aware of your feelings. Listen, touch, and see. Be deliberate. Observe your internal state, both physically and emotionally. Keep a fluid relationship between yourself and your surroundings.

Every moment should be seen as the sum of your entire life. Do not focus on the past or the future. Live here and now.

Trust yourself. Your heart and soul contain the energy of the universe. They are innately synchronized at birth. You must maintain this unity between the self and the universe. *Forever Now* is a practice that helps you do this. The dynamic relationship between the internal and the external is a life-long journey of awareness. The tools *Forever Now* provide help you uncover the purity of self. Living your life guided by your truthful spirit is the only way you can ever find ultimate tranquility, joy, and fulfillment.

Anything else can wait but your continued journey toward awakening cannot. Now is the time. If it's not now, when?

Printed in the United States
123383LV00003B/2/P